THE LAUGHTER OF THE SPHINX

ALSO BY MICHAEL PALMER

BOOKS AND CHAPBOOKS

Thread
Company of Moths
Codes Appearing
The Promises of Glass
The Danish Notebook
The Lion Bridge: Selected Poems 1972–1995
At Passages
An Alphabet Underground
For a Reading
Sun
Songs for Sarah
First Figure
Notes for Echo Lake
Alogon
Transparency of the Mirror
Without Music
The Circular Gates
C's Songs
Blake's Newton
Plan of the City of O

SELECTED TRANSLATIONS

Voyelles by Arthur Rimbaud
Jonah Who Will Be 25 in the Year 2000 (film by Alain Tanner)
The Surrealists Look at Art (with Norma Cole)
Blue Vitriol by Alexei Parshchikov (with John High and Michael Molnar)
Theory of Tables by Emmanuel Hocquard
Three Moral Tales by Emmanuel Hocquard
in *The Selected Poetry of Vicente Huidobro*
in *The Random House Book of Twentieth Century French Poetry*
in *Nothing the Sun Could Not Explain: 20 Contemporary Brazilian Poets*
in *Twenty-two New French Writers*

OTHER

Code of Signals: Recent Writings in Poetics, ed. Michael Palmer

MICHAEL PALMER

THE LAUGHTER OF THE SPHINX

A NEW DIRECTIONS BOOK

ACKNOWLEDGMENTS: Many of these poems first appeared in the following publications: *The American Reader, The Brooklyn Rail, Hambone, The Harvard Advocate, Lana Turner, The Ocean State Review, Phoebe, Plume, Spacecraftproject, Vanitas,* and *White Stag Review.*

Manufactured in the United States of America
New Directions Books are printed on acid-free paper
First published as New Directions Paperbook 1342 in 2016

Library of Congress Cataloging in Publication Data
Names: Palmer, Michael, 1943– author.
Title: The laughter of the sphinx / Michael Palmer.
Description: New Directions Publishing : New York, [2016]
Identifiers: LCCN 2016006852 | ISBN 978-0-8112-2554-0 (softcover : acid-free paper)
Classification: LCC PS3566.A54 A6 2016 | DDC 811/.54—dc23
LC record available at http://lccn.loc.gov/2016006852

10 9 8 7 6 5 4 3 2 1

New Directions Books are published for James Laughlin
by New Directions Publishing Corporation
80 Eighth Avenue, New York 10011

Contents

STILL

THE LAUGHTER
OF THE SPHINX

Author's Note

A number of the poems included here have led parallel lives. "Light Moves (1–6)" were written as one part of my collaboration with the Margaret Jenkins Dance Company on the dance *Light Moves* (2011). They pointedly echo and evolve from Jackson MacLow's *22 Light Poems* (Black Sparrow Press, 1968). Both "Sounds for *Times Bones*" and "Prose for *Times Bones*" were written for the same company's 40th-anniversary work, *Times Bones* (sic - 2014). "A Dream of Sound Inside the Mountain" was commissioned as a response to Anish Kapoor's sculpture "Large Mountain" and was first published as one in a series of responses by an international group of poets, a chapbook entitled "Poetry for Anish Kapoor" (Palais des Beaux-Arts, Bruxelles; Bozar Literature, 2013). "Let Us Ravel the Silence" first appeared in the French magazine *Ligne* 13 (#6, Winter-Spring 2013), in Françoise de Laroque's translation. It was published in conjunction with Irving Petlin's "The Emperor's Bridge," to which it is, similarly, a response. Petlin's pastel itself derives from an illustration in W. G. Sebald's *The Rings of Saturn*. So the wheel turns.

"Still" was conceived as an open sequence both for voices and for the page. The order of the poems need not be seen as fixed. I envisioned it with the possibility of musical accompaniment, hence performance. Should a composer ever care to take all or some of it on, I would hope that she or he would feel free to consider a transformative approach to the texts (e.g., by employing repeats, etc.) as desired. Here too, the possibility of parallel lives.

Idiot Song

By permission of the sun,
the arctic chill descends.

In a teacup a storm,
in a sentence the logician's fate

and poetry an enemy of the state
of things

by the roadside in a ditch
or beneath a buckled bridge.

Now it is our wounds
that make love in the streets,

wounds hastily dressed
with vetiver and mint

while slender poplars bend
amidst the violent winds.

What is your name,
mindless sun?

What idiot song
will mark your end?

Let Us Ravel the Silence

Let us ravel the silence,
its pages turning

It is a hum, after all, of no sound,
a buzz of absent bees,

a swirl of sky licked by flame
and a waste of sea,

reeds bending east towards a tentative shore,
scatter song of light's passage

across a curving earth
There is a bridge in the bare distance

It is a bridge between silences,
bridge of steel where once

the Emperor's dragon was meant to pass
bearing the palaces of the gods on its back,

brows furled over blazing eyes,
scales of gold coating the torso

And always the stones at sea-bottom
like extinguished stars

The sun here neither rises nor sets
Does chalk emit a breath

For László K

The characters are the victims of the novel
They pay with their lives
for our words
They fall between the pages
in their silence
and we invent hounds
to devour them
We invent worlds
to swallow them
We pass sentence
upon them
The hangman arrives
with his silken rope
its infinite strands
forming a circle
without beginning or end
round as the wave's grey eye
rolling toward what sudden shore
unpeopled yet teeming
with watchful night fires

The Laughter of the Sphinx

The laughter of the Sphinx
caused my eyes to bleed

The blood from my eyes
flowed onto that ancient map

of sand
Ridiculous as I am

often have I been drawn
to such lands

rippling oceans of silence
and the distant, enigmatic glow

of burning shops and burning scrolls
overseen by river birds and mitered beasts

sad-eyed scholars and mournful scribes
omniscient ibises

and in the dust-clogged air
the laughter of the Sphinx

endlessly riddling, endlessly echoing,
loosing the blood's engulfing tide

His Artificial Lover Sings a Wordless Song

The year of silence coming to an end
my artificial lover joined me on the fevered wheel

to the tune of Tinkers Polka, Plums of Purity,
Under the Double Eagle, When

the White Magnolias Bloom ...
Artificial love was in flower

amidst the revolutionary fragments.
I wondered then, do captive griffins roar

in their dreams? The Mosquito Waltz,
Tiger Mourning for Its Shadow ...

Far from the real
a day of naked beauty, filtered light.

Do children link their arms as before?
Do they play at rounders, blindman's buff?

Will the despoilers have it all
to themselves? Even the textured sky?

Xi Chuan, we often ask the same
questions it seems, or is it simply

that together we studied the stars
in Mechanicsville? Orion's Belt shown,

the Sisters and the Drinking Gourd.
Words formed

their own
seamless patterns

one moment,
sundered the next.

My artificial lover joined me on time's wheel
in the painted world.

The birds of the hours
crossed and recrossed

before us.
The crowded barques set out.

Isle of Dogs

On the Isle of Dogs we barked.
We had our say
from day till dark.

A chorus we were
of piebald hounds.
Our howling spiraled out

across the downs.
We howled at the redness of light,
bayed at the rising waters

and approaching night—
we lived on an island of sounds.
None listened, none heard,

the sounds were entirely ours .
None listened, none heard
but we didn't care

as long as our howls
shaped the still air—
we lived on the Isle of Sounds.

Light Moves 1

Mineral light and whale light,
light of memory, light of the eye,
memory's eye, shaded amber light
coating the page, fretted
light of anarchy, flare of bent
time, firelight and first light,
lake light and forest light,
arcing harbor light,
spirit light and light of the blaze,
enveloping blaze,
century's fading light,
light of cello, voice, drum,
figures billowing along
horizon, aligned, outlined.

Light Moves 2

Bright light of sleep, its
shortness of breath, its
thousand sexual suns, curved
and fretted light, lies of that light,
dark, inner light, its
whispered words:
Now beyond, now below,
this to left, this to right,
scarecrow in stubble field,
nighthawk on wire,
these to cleanse your sight.

Light Moves 3

Light through the Paper House
rippling across floors and walls,
across the words of the walls,
its paper tables, paper chairs,
its corners,
pale light by which it reads itself,
fills and empties itself,
and speaks.

Light Moves 4

Watcher on the cliff-head
in afternoon light, aqueous light,
watcher being watched
in the salt-silver light
amidst the darting of terns,
beach swallows and gulls,
between the snow of sand
and the transit of clouds,
keeper of thought or prisoner of thought,
watcher being watched,
snowman of sand,
anonymous man.

Light Moves 5

Night-sun and day-sun
twinned and intertwined,
light by a bedside,
cat's eye by night,
owl light and crystal light,
endless motion of the light,
the rise and the fall,
the splintered flare,
churning northern lights,
phosphor, tip of iris,
gunmetal moon's
far, reflected light,
oil sheen
on pelican's wing.

Light Moves 6

And yet what have we done
where have we gone
sometimes in light sometimes not
traveling
we say the great world the small world
the fields
patched with yellow the sudden crows
the city's streets
alone among others
the billowing streets
bodies crowding past
outlined by light.
What have we done
among the roads and fields
in the theater's shadows and the theater's light
so bright you cannot see
those watching beyond
in perfect rows in the dark.

(in homage to Jackson MacLow)

Untitled
(27 vii 2012)

A messenger passed over me
(it was 11:41 PM)
and I thought:
I wish I were as stark
and true as Sonny Rollins
those nights on the singing bridge,
wish to gnaw on the singing bones
in Charlieville and Rome,
wish for the peace of the blaze,
peace of the parricide,
of the eternal ferryman
blind to the river's twin sides.

A messenger passed over me
(it was 11:43).
I washed the last dishes,
gazed at my altered eyes
in the fractured glass,
found fellowship with a moth
flecked with gold,
tore certain pages apart.

A messenger passed over me
(it was 11:51).
I watched the rain
seep through the roof,
counted the drops,
thinking of Li Po.

A messenger passed through me
(it was 11:58),
passed over the waters
of the warming world,
passed through the eaves, the walls,
the pages of this house,
and I knew that soon enough I would become
a fossil bird or a diorite stone.

Trio (Paris 1959)

And at the Blue Note
that night Bud called
Pork Chops and Assholes

In Elegy
(The Mute Carter Sings)

Sings:
When young
we lived in a certain
enveloping light
and things turned
it seemed
toward our eyes
as if coming to be

Yet to see them again
as if ourselves then

The quartzite
stone the blood
pours through how
it pours silently through
the bright stone

The pepper tree that speaks
of lost meanings by a stream
meanings of speech
meanings of tree
what meaning to the stream

Wheels on the night path
sounding their way
The mute carter sings:
My cart is full
my cart is empty
one and the same

The voices of children
and dogs intermingling
the slender girls along the shore
chanting the coming mysteries
the confounding mysteries
of what is to be

In elegy the mirror
reassembling its shards

In elegy memory
embracing its shadows

In elegy shadows
refashioning the body

In elegy the bell
betraying the hours

In elegy the page
borne off by a breeze

The mute carter sings:
We swallow the earth

limb by limb
We pry open its

head to peer in
cut out its heart

sever its sex
to dissect to possess

The mute carter sings
by night of such things
along the way

His cart is full
his cart is empty
one and the same

Tomb of Aimé Césaire

I mourned a person who turned out
not to be dead
Of that what is to be said

Surgical noise of the city
Sentence and song under earth

I wept for something lost
a dawn or a dusk or a thought
a thing that couldn't be bought

Sun throat cut
Woman removing a glove

And the body at once naked
and veiled
waiting and waiting for what

Coma Berenices above the bay
sea wrack beneath

Speech of the bone
and of the polychrome wing
speech of the leaf descending

and of the rubble in a ruined field
Words have their lives apart

I mourned a person who turned out
not to have died
between a feral sky

and a flooded shore where
a wave was frozen in mid-air

Sounds for *Times Bones*
(among the dancers)

Such as we are, entering
Such as we are, in place, moving in place
Such as we are, departing

As we were as we are
As a leaking roof floods the stage
we become swimmers, waders

As the power fails
we sing Dancing in the Dark
In the dark

a rabbit leaps out of a hat,
a top hat,
clowns emerge from a tiny car,

countless clowns
numerous as stars
in the cartoon sky,

the invisible night sky
In the dark
the past crosses the stage

sipping from an emerald cup
and the night sun dances,
the day moon dances,

star throwers dance
in the ancient stone
Stones in the stream

roll drunkenly,
beheaded Orpheus, Orpheus unsexed
sings in the stream,

Osiris in the Atef crown
gathers up his limbs
Mosquitoes dance

The Man with Two Bodies, the Bearded Lady ...
The King of Pentacles
and the Queen of Wands ...

The Joker dances,
the Hanged Man,
the Knight and the Page

The Book of Hours dances in solitude,
so, and the green of serpentine,
the cliff swallow, the adamant child,

the echoing crowds
amid the burning buildings
in the streets and public squares

And at a certain moment, so,
the Ice Queen begins to dance
frozen in place

each stare, each gesture precise,
never a smile
She is the Queen of Ice

there where past and present
become perfectly aligned
as if beyond time

And she sings
"To begin is to begin to end"
And so time dances,

the body of time,
the bones sculpted by time
wobble and dance

and time's eyes watch,
watch as the seas rise,
laugh as the seas rise,

and the speakers are silent
though the words speak themselves
and the net of nerves

trembles, dances
as it did and as it will,
and the syllables

dance in The Devil's Dictionary,
the naked letters dance
They cannot know what tale they tell

in the dark, entering
such as they are, departing,
moving, moving through a place

that is moving, the players,
the few and the many,
feeling their way

Storm

Basho by my bedside
these many years

Little wonder
the roof is leaking

(for R.H.)

Unter den Linden

A visitor passing
gazes at the silence
between the cordate leaves
of the lime trees
along that avenue where once

And then among the leaves
wind-scorched, tremorous
a swell of bird song
saying nothing at all
to the visitor passing

(Berlin June 2012)

In Memory of Ivan Tcherepnin

So many sounds flower but they are not flowers.
They are mangled girders in a field,
a field of flowers, echo of hooves,
heavy-metal of tanks,
music's lost memory.

In the enveloping mist
our shoes squealing
upon the paving stones
while winding through
your Paris streets,
which one of us said,
The absolute
secret of art
lies in the tongue
of a shoe?
Who said, The true
secret of art
resides in the gaze
of a cat,
and that's that?
Which one of us asked,
Is this the buried sound
of the future-past?
Do electrons still sing
when no one is listening?
(A little stoned perhaps?)
We spoke of corpses
waving batons, hierophants
professing poems,
as the mist cloaked our words
and mid-summer night
measure by measure
finally arrived.

Ivan Alexandrovich,
is it only the fugitive things
that ravel the cells
and ring through the air,
le va et le vient as you put it,
the slow rise of a half-step,
followed by falling semi-tones,
in a day of one birth and one death?

So many sounds flower but they are not flowers.
They are street calls and cries
and the promises of bone,
and the bright sightless eye
at the flower's brief heart.

Call

Call it paradise or end-of-days
voiceless either way—the brief
though long-seeming dream

We scan the high plains, Elena,
for the fevered travelers
weary, onyx-eyed
travelers in caravans
bearing guns and gold
bright promises of jade
scented oils and healing herbs
pelts of elk and bear
and—strange to our ears—
the high-pitched, quavering
songs in exotic tongues
perhaps canticles of desire or lamentation
prayers perhaps that the journey end well
that darkness and light find their balance
in the passage from dark to dark

So the severed words rang out
in the gathering dark
as the figures disappeared
beyond the faint arc
of the indescribable world

Goes on goes gone came the thought:
salt sands boundary stones nebulae
ferrous cliffs bone beds solar discs

And there it ends, Elena,
"a scene or dream with no meaning"
so the silent dream insists
night birds passing
all glimpsed through a clouded lens

Now it is I
who cannot grasp a pen

Encounter

nelle parole
che incontra
non trova
che frammenti

giovanna sandri, from *incontro*

Together we walked
beneath a field
of stars effaced
in a city
strange to both

We spoke
a third language
not knowing
the other's first
Our nearness

such as it was
grew thus
in a shared distance
a dome of limbs
net of tongues

We apportioned
each to each
the mild night
the random calls
the thread of thought

Among the shuttered bookstalls
by the embankment
we passed
hand to hand the halves
of broken coins

the one from the future
one the past
and the one
coin unmoored from time
the last

Call the Makers

Call the makers before they're gone
Tell them

It ain't worth the candle
ain't worth a song

Untitled
(Jerusalem April 2013)

A poem (since that's
what it called itself)
left me behind at the Damascus Gate
It was it said one of a kind
It rained dry rain within this poem
at the gate of stone
and snowed a snow of burning words
with ancient scars at their hearts

The gate opened and the gate came closed
opened and endlessly closed
even through those nightly dreams
when the women of the song approached
one by one
to offer here a silken limb
there a sidelong glance or searing thought

My dictionary held no word for snow
no word for song or stone
My dictionary startled me with its gaze
as the children by the gate
sang in an unknown tongue
of a man so very very old
who once had a farm and a field
in the chalk-colored valley below
a field of olives and date palms and goats

The children chanted ee-aye-ee-aye-o
ee-aye-ee-aye-ee-aye
ee-aye-ee-aye o riven sky
their voices sounding across the valley floor
They sang hello good-by

I left a poem behind at the Damascus Gate
It was it said one of a kind
I swore to return sometime
though I knew it would be gone

Shrine
(Hong Kong)

The plastic
bodhisattvas
outnumbered us
on the climb
to enlightenment

Did

Did she seduce him
with her knowledge of Greece
and each of its islands

Did he seduce her
with compliments
about the taste of her tears

Their discussion
of the *Ars amatoria*
went very well

Their discussion
of the *Ars amatoria*
proceeded badly

Their words
grew heated
then chilled

A sudden sound
from outside
startled her

A sudden sound
from outside
excited him

A night bird possibly
with the yellowest of eyes
and slowly rowing wings

Did she say then
only when the two
have become one

do they discover
the absolute
invisibility of the other

even as their throats fill
with the salt syllables
of the other

Amber-eyed owl
all the while
keeping time

Untitled
(27 vi 2013)

Unwording—
he thought—

the page
swept clean

Prose for *Times Bones*

We all wanted a song and the song could mean anything ...

We all wanted a song and the song might mean nothing ...

Might sound between dream and waking ...

Might carve a body out of autumn air, the leaves coloring, bowing to time ...

What do we make of it, the tango of our thoughts over time, the arabesque, the Great Wall and the message wall, the walls being built and the walls falling, the wall of memory with its glimpses and crumbling stones ...

The fault lines in Prague, the formalities in Tokyo, the Chicago winds, the blistering heat and bone-deep cold, the moments grasped and the moments lost, the several bodies as one and the one as many ...

Sometimes the streets would be empty ...

Sometimes crowds would gather along the avenues and in the public squares, and they too would chant and they too would dance, and the walls would open and the moment become clear ...

And the tale?

Of the shorebirds and the salt breeze? The sound of Miss Jacobi's tears? And what of those other birds, large and small, flamboyant and plain of feather, gathering at the city gates, the rustle of their wings, was that twenty years ago? Can we imitate again their calls, their darting and gliding, their settling to earth, their love-making and quarrels? Does the kingfisher on a wire tell a tale? Does the osprey's cry? Do the pigeons in the bell-tower mark time? Do the whisperers still whisper over the years? Sometimes even a kettle will sing and often the waters will dance: the Vltava, the Rhine, the Tiber, the Seine, the Missouri, the Hudson, the Neva and the Wye ...

These waters that we've sat beside; these waters that we've crossed. And the machines of industry, the machines of war: their song, their dance? And so, where lies the tale? In the curl of an arm? The arching of a back? A glance? A leap or a turn? A thought carved in air? The emptiness of space itself, shaped only by light? Shaped only by silence? We take a breath, take a step, then another. So the tale. Told. Untold.

A Dream of Sound Inside the Mountain
(after Anish Kapoor)

It is too brief
this life
inside the mountain

where headless horsemen sing
fevered songs
of self and war

When did we first notice
the trees of mottled bone,
when first hear

the cawing of crows,
contention
of the orchard orioles,

the sleepers' echoing cries,
rehearsing their final words,
resisting final dreams

(These dreams were mine
and not mine
say the walls of stone,

walls of the poem)
Hedge-crickets sing
and the white whale

its whiteness sings
in the stone dream
and the lost hours have each

their silent song
in the heat of bee time
and the shock of desire

those times when time is not
and the endlessly shifting stones
carelessly speak

and rain floods the rutted roads
It is too long
this spiral life

It is too brief
How the wind and light pass
through our bodies of glass

Perfezione della neve

Teach me the secrets of that
language you speak
I entreated
her

Honor
(O.M.)

Honor
the poison
of the almond

Untitled
(15 viii 2013)

While dying
you grew

as translucent
as bone china

and your mind took flight
through space and time

as minds
should always do

Song

Festival night
We climb the candle one last time

The wind from the west
knows us best

We climb the candle
one last time

Blood-streaked horses
flare across the dream

They know us best
who know us least

The waters rise
as high as the flame

They are a test
And this text -

and this text I live in
is a difficult one

she mentioned in the dark
as we spoke

of syllables and suns
and sightless horses on the run

Festival night
We climb

a final time
and if it is a song

it is a song
not to be sung

Let Us

Let us
write without meaning
to

All

All the secrets of my work
reside
in the languages I have forgotten

I can't remember
who it was
whispered this to me

At the Tomb of Artaud

At the tomb of Artaud
wherever it may be
we hear a howl, unmistakable,
the howl of a wounded wolf
gnawing at its foreleg
caught in the teeth

of a hunter's steel trap
At the tomb of Artaud
wherever it may be
a sleeper and his double
throw dice made of bone
Should the dice fall

just so, they explain
it will snow
on the tomb of Artaud
Should they fall
otherwise
the earth will be dry

A dancer and her double
make love
on *the bright stones*
the light bringers
by the tomb of Artaud
that has become a book

of stone
they care not to read
whatever it may mean
as the fitful
iridescent
dragonflies alight

on the wet heat
of their bodies
Only later
will they piss on his grave
as a clock without hands
applauds in the dark

Poem
(Oct – Nov 2013)

It is true that we write
with one eye toward dying,
true that we write
with a blind eye,
eye blinded by a shadow
cast across the sun
or by a fictive glimpse
of the beloved. It is true
that we do not write,
that a measureless silence
writes in our place
of all it surveys
and cannot say, the phosphorous
rain, the lies of the prophets,
the table set for dinner
in a suddenly deserted house
of stone. What wild
storm swept them away, what
thing unforeseen, implements,
full pitchers and plates
still carefully arrayed
as if an evening meal
were always to come.
It is true that as we write
our skin grows transparent,
our bones brittle
and the words take leave
of what they'd thought to mean.
The scent of bay and mint
lingers nonetheless
by the scorched field's
jagged edge
where in the jagged moment
nothing's to be said.

To X
(*Endarkenment*)

Who is the night creature
that devoured the clover,

who the mathematician
who first solved to X?

The child lost in the house
in the dark corridors of the house

endless corridors of the house,
what child, what house?

Those blood-red nasturtiums—
I planted them for Arkadii

when I heard of his death
having forgotten

that I was not, not ever,
in this echoic life

to mention death
either of the self or the other,

the particle or the page
curled at its edges

by what random flame?
It is no match for the flame

to which the lovers are consigned
no match for the wind

that feeds the flame
no match for the fate

of the earth at our hands.
It is complex

the mathematics of lovers
where one plus one

equals what?
And the lost child

for who was not once
the lost child

and who will not
become so again?

By the River of the Fathers
we often gathered as kids.

It stank of chemicals and shit,
not the river's fault,

not your fault, not mine,
a sacred, baptismal river, Arkadii,

your book has arrived
though you've suddenly left.

for Zina

To the Polish Poets
(March 2014)

This watch
carved it would appear
from a solid
titanium block
sits comfortably on the wrist
even magisterially—
a corrupt, despicable word—
magisterially nonetheless
and impervious to the elements
as advertised.
It is what the children
of the present age
call scornfully
a dedicated device
serving no purpose
other than the seconds
the minutes the hours
rendered in analogue
no indicators for a coming storm
or a great wave approaching
the ever crumbling coast
or for the earth as it shifts
suddenly beneath us
no indicators
for the first veiled light
of dawn
and the seabirds'
accompanying swarms.
Impassive of face
free of memory free of time
this block.

A Late Supper

In a digital dream
it is always one in the morning.

Asger Jorn and my father
sit at the dining room table

discussing hotel management
with Marcel Duchamp

who has just coined the phrase,
"Dinner is not served."

Salt cellar, pepper grinder, candles,
the roasted head of a goat

and a vintage bottle of red
from Ceauşescu's private stash,

liberated upon his death.
My pen. My pen is leaking ink,

Nicolae, and these flowers are wilting
though freshly cut.

Cavafy would approve, I suspect,
of the flowers if not the goat

were he here now,
but he never leaves his room.

Poem Devoid of Meaning

We turn our heads away
from the three-headed lady

We avert our gaze
from the lizard-limbed one

the feathered one
in her wire cage

and Thimble Boy sipping
his smoked China tea

We exchange warm greetings
with the world's tallest man

(a friend of my father
across the distant years)

a giant named Saul
who has just days

to live and no more
An announcement is made:

the captain has abandoned ship
and only minutes remain

Somewhere I once read
that anyone can pilot a ship

through raging waters
should he demonstrate

clarity of mind
and purity of heart

I have removed my heart
and placed it on the deck

the better for all to examine it:
tell-tale signs of wear

among the valves
and significant rust

along the vena cava
traces of mercury

and a hint of cesium
in the left anterior

Fellow passengers shut tight their eyes
except for the three-headed lady

who notes, It is good, good enough,
mon semblable, mon frère, sail on

Strange Now

Strange now to find ourselves
in these later, lateral days,
to lose ourselves in this slowing time
of a late, lateral light,
a slant, abbreviated light
knowing that we all, each one,
once thought to become
waves beating, waves retreating,
wheeling, oval eyes of storm,
swallow-tales, atoms of thought,
as if there were such things
as if such things could be
could have been

We do know
that the cry
concerns no one at all
Someone first said this
at song's dark antipodes,
not one of my friends
in the Brazil of endless song,
not the poet of brilliant,
invisible colors
who despairs of her work,
never ceases to mourn,
not the Cape Verdean singer
to whom I sent a kiss
across uncharted waters,
a kiss graciously acknowledged,
night is such,
not

Icarus, not the cardinal
emerging in fire from the dense,
sugar-scented
privet, not a memory

of gentle hills
invented to please
or console, we borrow
a letter from dawn,
one from dusk,
one from the sun,
one from the sudden
rain, one last
from the howling of dogs
and claim
that this sudden alphabet
is ours

Falling Down in America

Every three seconds someone over sixty-five
falls down in America.
Our records show
that you are over sixty-five
and may therefore have already
fallen down in America
maybe more than once.
Perhaps upon entering your bath
you slipped
and cracked open your skull
and subsequently drowned
in a pool of blood.
If so, disregard this notice.
Perhaps while gazing at the sea
distractedly one day
your balance failed
and the waves carried you away
toward the irradiated swells
of Fukushima.
If so, never mind—
the flesh has already peeled
from your limbs
and your eyes
have melted in their sockets
in which case
you should disregard this notice.
We need hardly remind you
that many of your friends
and relatives, perhaps beloved uncles,
aunts, cousins, your seven brothers
and sisters, parents assuredly,
may have succumbed in some manner
to the fateful equation
of gravity and age.
In addition, it is likely
that your investments recently caved

and as a result, from the shock,
you fainted upon the cheap
Mexican tiles
of your dining room floor
and days later awoke
among impersonal professionals,
masked and clad in white,
and addressing you
as if you were a child.
If so, you now know
that you are utterly alone
in this life.
Please favor us with a reply
regarding our one-time offer
which will soon expire.

Proposition

To write as perfectly as Euclid
was always the goal
even as he turned out
to be perfectly wrong.
The stars are not above

but somewhere within
and following from this
no lines are straight
no beginnings no ends
and the drought-dry streams

parch our voices
so that songs of dust
billow forth
and betray the lovers' trust.
Beside this world another

orphaned from time
where darkness and light
dance on a turtle's back
and rage at each other in rhyme.
Beneath this world another

precise mirror of our own
where chaos is abiding law
and memory nothing at all.
Follows the careening world
world of clown cars and thought balloons

of hat tricks and punch lines
where comedian-philosophers
the funniest of women and men
and the most blessed
hang themselves hourly

among the orderly rows
of ice-bright almond trees
as if to cause laughter to freeze
for the remainder of time.
There they become

the fruit of such gods
as do not appear
and never speak
those who laugh silently
at the very idea

of cones and primes
angles and spheres
motion and rest
atoms and amulets.
Your words ever perfect, mad Euclid.

Addendum

Needless to say, as we now know—or always knew—there are infinite worlds beyond, or beside, or within that of Euclid, far too many to measure or to name. For example, there is the world of the Mute Queen, whose subjects must never speak, lest she thereby discover her disability. And the parallel world of silence, well-known to poets, where only the space between words signifies and words themselves are empty, no more than sounds echoing in the still air. And in another world, still another, there is no present, nothing but the past. We are what has been. We loved, we made love, we sang, we composed new songs, we danced in the bodies that were ours, laughed then, fought pointless wars, pillaged, gloried in it all, gazed at a stream that was, a city on a hill, a shining city that was, where is is no more.

Et in Arcadia

It rained frogs.
We were the frogs
and the rain.

As the planets fled their orbits
apples ripened
in the orchards to our north.

We bit into the planets
as if they were apples.
They crackled

between our teeth
and their juices
streamed off our jowls

like syllables from childhood.
Our mad brothers, mad
lovers, mad others

were already gone.
The bees and their hexagons,
their dances, were gone,

the whales and their songs.
Shoeless we walked
across the stellated,

the glowing, irradiated
meadows of glass.
Have you always

had this tremor?
she asked.
Yes.

The Republic

They bellow, these silent
creatures of the carousel,

these dragons and centaurs,
unicorns and sea-beasts,

and always the horses,
dappled, candy-striped, pure white.

Their eyes are ablaze
with what they cannot see,

ablaze with the thoughts
they cannot think.

They cannot think
of the spinning world

in which they turn.
They cannot hear

the music they encircle
pouring from the pipes

of the wheezing calliope,
its melodies bent by the wind

into the semitones
of an unintended world.

And the children, the wild
children as they ride,

laugh in their pleasure
and in their terror

at a slow-dawning knowledge
that the beasts will devour them.

After

And to write a poem
beneath the sickle moon
is barbaric

And to trace a poem
upon the lover's body
is barbaric

And to write a poem
amidst the dust
amidst the dust

storm of history is barbaric
And to read a poem
To read

while the book is burning
and to enter the Paper House
while the streets are burning

To enter the Paper House
which is silent
And to hear the song

should we call it a song
soonest gone
of the cicadas

in the parching heat
when to drink
of the lover's liquid

is barbaric
And to wander
in a dark wood

wander lost
in a dark wood
to look

and to begin
to say farewell
to begin

and to dwell
to dwell upon
to dwell among

STILL

(A CANTATA—OR NADA—
FOR SISTER SATAN)

Zeit ist Geld
as we say in America

and art too
buckle my shoe

to the wall
my heart to my jaw

my throat to the kestrel's cry
Call me Digital Mike

or Mnemonic Mike
or Felonious Mike

or even better
don't ever call

Time is money
says it all

1st chorus

And the children, who have no language,
sing:

obatai roma obatai
romatai oba romatai

They sing *lee la lee*
in pursuit of light

And the children, who have no knowledge
of death

sing with their darting hands
offer praise in the stubble fields
turn their faces to greet the rain

And the children, with their knowledge of death,

place sound upon sound
stone upon stone
fire upon flame

They pour sand on their heads
They bow toward the west

obatai roma obatai

                                          "There's no
                               more to say"
                                        –Inger Christensen

There's no there's no there's no
more to say

There are the minutes the hours
the pulses of the day

There are day lilies, cormorants, fretted clouds
There are the sweet smells of baking,

apples tart and mild
along the way

There is a chair of solid oak
You sit on it to write

You get up and pace
and it is late, the light

is gone, there's a drunk
muttering by the curbside

about eyes, Why so many
eyes

ancient, babbling child, swollen,
tattered, rheumy-eyed

once hazel perhaps, hazel-eyed,
why so many hours, so many eyes

There's no there's no there's no
more to say, there's a chair

of solid oak, a desk
where you sit to write,

scent of night jasmine,
memory of a face, a voice,

body taut, short of breath, des-
perate dancer

grasping for air, never, not
ever quite enough, actias

luna, luna moth, desperately
dancing toward light, not ever

quite enough
and the page

upon the desk is white,
the desk, as it happens,

the improvised desk
also white

the plum blossom
and the night sky at times

almost white
and as to the children

erased this day
beneath a placid sky

beneath a phosphorus rain
a rain white as night

along the sandy shore
where they'd slipped away to play

for a time (Can
you tell us the time,

Venus-Phosphor, Morning Star?)
they will be long

forgotten by tomorrow
We will remember to forget them

We will be certain
to forget them

since it's necessary
that there be no more to say

The child first learning the words
wonders what comes between the words.
And learning the words she tries to recall
what came before,
a ringing or whistling or roaring, a
kind of chorus perhaps, as of wind over water,
like the water here, near enough to see
that's mysteriously called the Sound.
Are there sounds between the words
where all feels asleep and still?
Maybe she laughs at the thought
that the words breathe too
and that the breathing turns
right there, in the air between the words.

2nd chorus

And the ancient children of stone,
the kouroi and the korai,

their bodies are still as they sing
of what has passed and what is to come

since they know too much
of binary stars and spots on the sun,

of the tyger in the night,
the tyger burning all too bright,

the forest, the anvil and the furnace,
and the sovereign secrets

of the tongue and of the bone,
the sovereign secrets

of tongue and bone.
To the mother they soundlessly sing

Are you here or are you gone?
And they see the father dazed,

mute singer as well, brittle and bent,
effaced by time's remains

and an elsewhere not to be named.
Sing, silent father, my brother,

in your distant tongue,
lost father, lost other.

Sing of the flesh and of the bone
and speak for the children of stone,

the kouroi and the korai
and the secrets of their smile.

From the broken tower
of the Cathedral of Our Lady
of the Holy Spectacle we watch
the rockets fall upon the small
and ever smaller figures.
They rain down in many colors,
chrome yellow, magenta, blood red
and a white whiter than white
before the attentive audience,
eager, fervent and intense
as if in a kind of trance.
The latest show
is always the greatest
until the next.

And the children sing
knowing and unknowing

in the space of the field
that is opening,

in the child's slow time,
the rhymes of the day

and the rhymes of night,
the rhymes of still water

and those of sudden fire,
of the lamb, the dolphin and the unicorn,

and the white spider constructing a cloud.
Say apple for the first time,

say yellow apple, wagon, plum,
sea horse, flying horse, river horse

and taste mint, say mint,
watch the lantern light as it plays

across the furred walls of a barn,
the curves of a rutted path,

words, so many, made for ears?
For eyes? So many eyes, say

I, say cyan, violet, wintergreen
beneath your feet, the simple

words as they vanish
among the white oaks'

echoing shadows, the paw paws, the
sassafras with lobed leaves,

the spirals of summer thought,
sing the secrets of the stream.

for Nico

Things get lost
things whose words
can no longer be heard

Still we try to find them
and place them
inside the silences

> The Emperor will get his cities,
> his drummer boy lie in the snow.
> —Marina Tsvetaeva

The children drum on anything
a bottle, a pan, the corpse of a car

They drum Sister Satan into the garden
They drum the dogs of war

loose upon the poppy fields
They drum whatever they can find

a skull will do, a smile, a wooden shoe,
most anything will do

these children
who are who they are

They drum the forest, the bones, the night
right up the Glass Mountain

They drum whatever they can find
They drum the silent sky

3rd chorus

And the elders as one:
I was sealed in the magic box

there to be taken
limb by limb apart

Invisible I danced
with Sister Satan

As regards her caress
you may only guess

At last I wore no mask
The seasons came the seasons went

seasons of our waking
seasons of our sleep

Where it was cold
now it was hot

Where rivers had flowed
nothing but sand

new world we had wrought
The shadows of mournful ancestors

passed across the sun
lighting that magic box

though I knew them not
Invisible we danced

Sister Satan and I
dismembered as we were

all torsos all legs all arms
still eager to please one another

while the clowns of our better natures
sang untranslatable songs